Beauty

Strengthen and care for your skin and body—from the inside

from Within

EAT YOUR WAY TO HEALTH AND BEAUTY

Beauty is more than simply having a good figure. Vitality and good health play an important part. Skin, hair, and nails are fortified by various vitamins and minerals that must come from the food we eat. Our digestive system releases them from what we consume, and our blood circulation transports them to where they are used. At the same time, the blood absorbs waste materials, carries them to the liver and kidneys for detoxification, and expels them. This process is essential, since our cells are constantly renewing themselves. The more smoothly this process of removal and renewal runs, the more beautiful you will become.

BUILDING BLOCKS OF NUTRITION

First of all, the food we eat is converted into energy, which is measured in kilocalories (commonly shortened into calories). The body "burns" this energy during metabolism, or uses parts of it as building blocks to regenerate itself.

These building blocks are:

* Carbohydrates, which are the principal component of fruit, vegetables, and grains. Carbohydrate-rich foods also provide fiber, water-soluble vitamins, and minerals. However, some carbohydrates also contain fast-releasing sugar, which, if eaten in excess, can make us tired and lethargic.

* Protein, which is considered a building block of our body's cells. It is present in enzymes, hormones, and antibodies, and carries our genetic materials. Protein is needed constantly for proper cell renewal. It is found in fish, meat, eggs, dairy products, cereals, and grains.

* Fat, which is a component of hormones and bile acids. It carries fat-soluble vitamins, and is a component of cell walls—and thus of our skin. Unsaturated fatty acids are vital to health, and are contained in good-quality, cold-pressed oils. The hidden fats in foods like meat products, cakes and cookies, though delicious, are tricky, and can contribute to the storage of excess fat deposits.

* Fiber, a substance that can help banish sluggishness. It consists of plant cellulose, which your body doesn't digest, so it contains no calories. Fiber is present mainly in fruit, vegetables, and grains. It ensures that waste products are quickly expelled from the body. Fiber also fills us up without leading to weight gain.

THE LITTLE THINGS
THAT MEAN A LOT

The body is unable to produce a lot of the active substances that monitor and control our metabolism; we need to absorb them from the food we eat. And although we need only the tiniest quantities of these substances, we often do not get enough of them. You can read more about this on the chart on the next pages.

* Minerals are the building blocks for bones, teeth, hair, and blood—but they also regulate the central metabolic processes, and maintain our inner balance.

* Vitamins are involved in all metabolic processes, and play a decisive role in processing foods in our diet; in other words, they help us to produce energy. Vitamins strengthen our immune system, regulate our mineral balance, and control cell regulation.

* Although so-called "bioactive" substances (phytochemicals, or plant chemicals) are not essential, they do play a key role in keeping us healthy and feeling good. They are created during the metabolic process of plants, so they are present in fruit, vegetables, and grains. Many bioactive substances not only help prevent circulatory problems and atherosclerosis (clogging of the arteries), but also protect the cells against environmental damage.

NUTRIENT	EFFECT
Vitamin D	Prevents osteoporosis by stimulating the body to absorb more calcium
Vitamin E	Antioxidant–protects against free radicals; keeps tissues elastic, stimulates the circulation
Vitamin B$_1$	Strengthens nerves and muscles
Vitamin B$_2$	Aids in protein metabolism, cell division, nervous system; combats PMS and morning sickness
Vitamin B$_{12}$	Essential for cell division and blood formation
Niacin	Promotes smooth skin and calm nerves; aids in energy utilization
Pantothenic acid	Promotes skin and hair renewal; aids healing
Folic acid	Promotes cell division and formation, formation of blood cells, immune system health
Iron	Aids in formation of blood cells, healthy skin, shiny hair, strong fingernails
Selenium	Contributes to healthy skin and nails; aids in detoxification
Zinc	Promotes strong hair and healthy skin; aids healing and the immune system; improves sensuality
Iodine	Contributes to proper function of metabolism; helps maintain a slim figure
Calcium	Forms strong bones, teeth, nails, and hair; benefits the nerves
Silicic acid	Firms tissues; strengthens skin and hair
Lactic acid	Beneficial to intestinal flora and the immune system; aids iron absorption
Omega-3-fatty acids	Aids circulation; helps maintain a healthy heart
Gamma-linoleic acid	Contributes to healthy, firm skin
Carotenoids	Boost the immune system; beta-carotene, a precursor of vitamin A, contributes to smooth, healthy skin

Found In

Oily fish, egg yolks, butter. Produced by the skin when exposed to sun

High-quality plant oils, especially wheat germ oil, fish, grains, and nuts

Whole wheat products, yeast, potatoes

Whole wheat products, fish, shellfish, cabbage, leeks, beans

Meat, fish, dairy products, foods containing lactic acid, yeast extract

Whole wheat products, meat, fish, potatoes

Liver, yeast, mushrooms, whole wheat products

Raw green vegetables, nuts, seeds, yeast, oranges, mangos

Meat, fish, millet, green vegetables, dried fruit, nuts

Fish (especially tuna and herring), whole grains, vegetables, mushrooms

Brewer's yeast, cheese, liver, nuts, sea vegetables, oysters

Shellfish, iodized salt, sea vegetables

Milk, yogurt, cottage cheese, tofu, collard greens

Whole grains, especially millet, oats, barley

Sauerkraut, pickled gherkins, yogurt, kefir, buttermilk, cheese, salami, olives, soy sauce

Oily fish (herring, salmon), flaxseed and canola oils

Plant oils (borage, sunflower, thistle, flaxseed), avocados, fish

Yellow, red, and green fruits and vegetables, such as apricots, winter squash, and broccoli

Beauty

everything for beauty

Basics

THE AMAZING POWERS OF NATURAL OILS

Though recent thinking has ruled fats unfavorable, we actually need them to stay alive. Plant oils contain many fats that are beneficial to our health and appearance. Cold-pressed plant oils retain more of sensitive substances and delicate aromas than heat processed oils. The following oils are especially beneficial:

* Black cumin oil*—contains polyunsaturated fatty acids and minerals that are effective against allergic and inflammatory symptoms. The oil has a spicy, Asian aroma.

* Borage oil*—contains a good amount of gamma linoleic acid, which is effective against eczema and general skin irritations. Use in moderation.

* Canola oil—also contains plenty of omega-3 fatty acids, and has a fresh flavor; a good choice for salad dressings and stir-fries.

* Flaxseed oil*—contains good amounts of omega-3 fatty acids. It's yellow in color, has a slightly bitter aroma, and goes well with strong flavors.

* Olive oil—consists mainly of monounsaturated fatty acids that prevent the arteries from clogging.

* Wheat germ oil*—contains an exceptionally high proportion of vitamin E, has a grainy-nutty flavor, and goes well in sweet dishes.

The oils listed above can be found in supermarkets or health-food stores, or from mail-order sources. Many are available from Internet suppliers.

*Store these valuable oils in the refrigerator, and use them within a few days. Bring them to room temperature and mix well before using.

WATER FOR FIRMNESS

Our bodies consist of at least two-thirds water, the amount of which decreases as we age. Water dissolves and transports the water-soluble nutrients in our body. It regulates the body's temperature and removes hazardous materials. Water makes the skin firm and smooth. For maximum benefit, our bodies need between 1.5 and 2 quarts of water a day—more in warm weather or if we are performing hard physical work or vigorous exercise.

Fresh from the Sea

Sea water contains lots of minerals, some of which are rare on dry land, such as iodine, iron, calcium, magnesium, fluoride, and zinc. Sea vegetables, mussels, oysters, and crustaceans filter these minerals out of the sea, and concentrate them.

* Nori (dried seaweed) is available roasted and formed into fine sheets. Nori is commonly used to make sushi. It is delicate, slightly spicy, high in protein, contains large amounts of vitamins A and C, and plenty of calcium and iron. Look for nori in a well-stocked supermarket or Japanese market.

* Sea vegetables provide many beneficial nutrients. Arame is a brown sea vegetable that is bursting with iodine and calcium. Arame contains more iron and vitamin B12 than meat, and is therefore ideal for a meat-free diet. Dulse is a type of red seaweed with many of the same qualities as arame. Before cooking, sea vegetables should be soaked in water for about 5 minutes, until they double in volume. Sea vegetables can be found in health food stores or Asian markets.

* Oily saltwater fish, such as salmon, tuna, mackerel, and herring, contain large amounts of highly beneficial omega-3 fatty acids. They also contain good quantities of protein and iodine.

* Shrimp, mussels, and oysters, are delicate reserves of zinc, iron, selenium, and fluoride.

Natural

for healthy-looking skin and shiny hair

Skincare

BALSAM FOR THE SKIN

Our skin breathes through the pores, where it eliminates waste products and absorbs beneficial substances. Cold-pressed oils, fruit, vegetables, milk, and other dairy products contain substances that effect the skin in a number of different ways. Below, find several masks made from fresh, natural ingredients, based on skin type. After mixing, apply to the face and neck, then cover with a moist cloth and relax for 20-30 minutes. The benefits are even greater if you can lie down and relax while the mask works. Rinse off the mask with plenty of lukewarm water, and apply a nourishing cream. These masks are gentle and can be safely applied once or twice a week.

PEACH MASK: FOR ANY SKIN TYPE

For best results, choose a ripe, fragrant peach. Peel and chop the peach, then mash with a fork.

AVOCADO MASK: FOR DRY SKIN

Peel 1 ripe avocado, and puree with a few drops of lemon juice and 1 teaspoon of borage oil.

CUCUMBER OR SAUERKRAUT MASK: FOR OILY SKIN

Wash and peel the cucumber, then grate it. Refreshes and smoothes the skin. You could also use freshly prepared sauerkraut (from a delicatessen), which is astringent and anti-inflammatory.

COTTAGE CHEESE MASK: FOR TIRED SKIN

Drain 3 tablespoons of low-fat cottage cheese, and combine with 1 tablespoon lemon juice, 1 tablespoon buttermilk, and 1 teaspoon wheat germ oil, stirring until the mixture is smooth.

SKINCARE FOR THE BODY

If you would like to do something to benefit the skin on your whole body, a combination of massage and bath is ideal. The temperature of the bath water should be between 98.6°F (body temperature) and 102°F. Do not spend more than 15-20 minutes in the tub. A bath that's too long and too hot will dry the skin rather than care for it.

While you are in the bath, soak a washcloth in the bath water and place it on your face. Do this several times. This opens the pores and helps to cleanse the skin. Good tip: after your bath, apply one of the beauty masks above and relax on the bed or couch for half an hour. Incidentally, cold-pressed oils, especially wheat germ, sesame, and olive oil, are wonderful for the skin—and contain no additives. Borage oil is especially good for dry, irritable skin.

Treat For Dry Skin
Before bathing, massage your whole body, from top to toe, with wheat germ oil, working from the extremities toward the heart. Then run your bath, adding 3 quarts of buttermilk or milk.

Purify Oily Skin
Stand in the shower and massage your body with wheat bran. Then, pour 2 cups of fruit vinegar into the bath water.

Nourish Your Hair
Your hair is nourished from the roots. Central heating, sun, and cold air are bad for the hair, turning it dry and brittle. Apply a strengthening pack from time to time—it works like magic. Wash your hair as you normally would, then apply the lukewarm pack to your hair, avoiding your scalp but paying particular attention to the roots. Then, put on a shower cap, wrap a towel around your head to keep it warm, and let the pack do its work for at least 1 hour. Afterwards, wash your hair thoroughly with a mild shampoo.

Herb and Oil Pack
Pour 1 1/4 cups of cold-pressed olive oil over 2-3 sprigs of fresh thyme, 1 sprig of fresh rosemary, and 1/2 handful of birch leaves (from a personal care or beauty supply store). Place the concoction in a cool, dark place for 1-4 weeks. Pass the oil through a strainer and squeeze out the herbs. Measure out the amount you need to cover your head before applying, then heat slightly.

Egg and Oil Pack
Depending on the length of your hair, beat 1-2 egg yolks with 1-2 teaspoons of cold-pressed wheat germ oil. Heat the mixture until lukewarm and rub into your hair.

Power

well-being and relaxation at home

Week

SPOIL YOURSELF!

You don't have the time or money for a week at a spa? Then spoil yourself at home using the recipes in this book. Do something for your body at the same time—go swimming, cycling, or jogging. Spend 15 minutes a day doing some exercise. And, as a special indulgence, treat yourself to a visit to the beauty salon. A massage followed by a steam bath or sauna will also do you good.

MINI SPA

Of course, you can't expect miracles in just a week, but it can be a new beginning.
In corporate some of the things you do in this week into your everyday life: drink lots of water, eat lots of fruit and vegetables, use a minimum of fat in your cooking—but make sure you do not miss out on the valuable fats. You will find that this short "cure" is a culinary delight. You will not be hungry: you can eat as many raw vegetables and berries, apples, and citrus fruit as you like for the duration of the week. But take care not to spend the whole day "grazing"— have three good meals a day, and maybe a snack in the morning or afternoon.

DRINK YOURSELF BEAUTIFUL

Drink as much herbal and green tea as you like. For best results, you can drink about two cups of ordinary tea and coffee per day, adding a little low-fat milk and cane sugar or honey—if you need it! Or, drink sparkling water, adding a splash of apple or lemon juice if desired. And what about alcohol? Well, it's bad news for your looks, but it can definitely add to a celebratory mood. For example, you can have a glass of dry Champagne to kick off your Power Week. But spare yourself on Sunday: make sure you get lots of sleep, go for a swim and a sauna, have a soak, and put a mask on your skin and a pack on your hair to motivate yourself for the week. That's not to say you must follow our suggestions to the letter: have a bowl of low-fat granola and a drink in the morning, then one cold and one hot main meal of your choice later in the day.

Eating Plan for the Week

Monday

- Buckwheat and Apple Granola
- Cabbage and Apple Salad
- Spicy Beef Stir-Fry with Avocado; 1 slice of whole wheat bread

Tuesday

- Mocha Milkshake; 1 slice of whole wheat bread
- Green Bean and Shrimp Salad; 1 slice of whole wheat bread
- Turkey Breast with Endive

Wednesday

- Citrus Muesli, Apple Cooler
- Choco-Risotto
- Boiled Potatoes with Creamy Power Spread

Thursday

- Melon Puree with Fruited Risotto; Orange-Scented Barley Water
- Dry-Cured Beef Sandwich
- Green Veggie Ragout

Friday

- Orange and Carrot Cottage Cheese
- Pesto-Mozzarella Sandwich
- Millet Spaghetti with Carrots

Saturday

- Six-Grain Granola with Fruit
- Fruited Cottage Cheese
- Chinese Fondue; Grapefruit and Carrot Salad

Sunday

- Fruit Salad with Grapes; Avocado-Fruit Drink
- Lime-Marinated Ceviche; fruit of your choice
- Artichokes with Avocado Dip; Lamb Cutlets with Vegetables

Avocado

light and creamy for

Fruit

a little extra energy

Drink

Serves 2: 1 small, soft avocado • 2 sprigs fresh lemon balm or mint • 1/4 cup fresh lemon juice • 1 1/4 cups pear juice • 1 tsp borage oil

Halve the avocado, remove the pit, and scrape out the flesh with a spoon. Wash and shake dry the lemon balm or mint, and remove the leaves from the stalks. In a blender, puree the avocado, lemon balm or mint leaves, lemon juice, pear juice, and borage oil. Dilute to taste with ice-cold water.

power

PER PORTION: 205 calories • 2 g protein • 13 g fat • 24 g carbohydrates

Orange-Scented

lifts the mood and counters water retention

Barley Water

Serves 2: 2 oz pearl barley • 1 1/2 quarts water • Juice of 1 orange

Rinse the barley well. Place it in a saucepan with the water and bring to a boil. Reduce the heat, cover tightly, and simmer for 30 minutes. Strain, saving the cooking liquid, and reserving the barley for another use. Let the liquid cool, then place it in the refrigerator until chilled. Combine the barley water with the fruit juice, and drink well chilled.

PER DRINK: 120 calories • 4 g protein • 1 g fat • 24 g carbohydrates

Mocha

detoxifies and aids digestion

Milkshake

Serves 2: 2 1/2 cups acidopholous milk • 1 tbs instant espresso • 1 tsp cocoa powder • 1 tsp bee pollen • 1 tbs oats • 2-3 tbs honey • 1 small banana (optional)

Combine the milk, espresso, cocoa powder, pollen, oats, and honey in a blender. Blend until the ingredients are smooth and dissolved. For a milder flavor and additional nutrients, blend in the banana.

PER DRINK: 85 calories • 3 g protein • 0 g fat • 19 g carbohydrates

Apple
cleanses from within
Cooler

Serves 2: 1 1/4 cups apple juice • 1 1/4 cups sparkling water • 1/4 cup cider vinegar • 1 tbs honey • 1 tsp bee pollen

Combine the apple juice, water, vinegar, honey, and bee pollen. Mix the ingredients well until everything is dissolved. It's best to sip this at room temperature.

PER DRINK: 100 calories • 0 g protein • 0 g fat • 26 g carbohydrates

power

Orange-Aloe
with lots of vitamin C and beta-carotene
Cooler

Serves 2: 6 tbs aloe vera juice • 1 1/2 cups freshly squeezed orange juice • 1 tsp borage oil • 1 tbs wheat germ

In a blender, combine the aloe vera juice, orange juice, oil, and wheat germ. Blend well at the highest speed, then pour into tall glasses and serve immediately.

power

PER DRINK: 137 calories • 3 g protein • 3 g fat • 26 g carbohydrates

Citus

stimulating and skin friendly

Muesli

Peel the grapefruit or oranges with a sharp knife, removing the white pith.

Slice the grapefruit or oranges into quarters, and remove the white

Serves 2:

1 pink grapefruit, or 2 oranges

1 small or 1/4 large fresh ripe pineapple

2 oz flaked millet

2 tbs wheat germ

1 tbs bee pollen

1/2 cup multivitamin juice

membrane from the middle. Cut the quarters into slices, collecting the juice.

Peel the pineapple, remove the brown "eyes," cut it lengthwise into quarters, and remove the core. Cut into bite-sized pieces, collecting the juice. Place the chopped fruit and juice, flaked millet, wheat germ, bee pollen, and multivitamin juice in a bowl, and mix. Divide the muesli among two dishes and serve.

Pineapple

Fresh pineapple contains large amounts of the enzyme *bromelin*, which breaks down protein. It is diuretic, sudorific, and cleanses the skin.

power

PER PORTION:

205 calories

5 g protein

2 g fat

42 g carbohydrates

Six-Grain Granola
with bioactive bee pollen
with Fruit

Serves 2: 8 dried apricots • 8 dried plums • 2 oz six-grain cereal • 2 1/2 cups acidopholous milk • 2 tbs honey • 2 tbs sesame seeds • 1 tsp bee pollen

Rinse the apricots and plums, and cut them into small pieces. Bring the cereal, dried fruit, and 1 1/2 cups of the milk to a boil in a saucepan. Remove from the heat, and stir in the honey and remaining 1 cup milk. Let the mixture cool. Stir in the sesame seeds and the bee pollen, and serve.

PER PORTION: 405 calories • 8 g protein • 4 g fat • 87 g carbohydrates

Buckwheat and
with lots of oats and yogurt
Apple Granola

Serves 2: 2 oz buckwheat groats • 2 apples • 2 tbs oat bran • 5 tbs oat flakes • 2 cups plain yogurt • 1 tsp borage oil • 3-4 tbs maple syrup

Toast the buckwheat in a dry nonstick skillet over medium heat, until you begin to smell it. Wash and dry the apples, then grate them coarsely (do not peel). Mix the grated apples with the oat bran, oat flakes, toasted buckwheat, yogurt, borage oil, and maple syrup. Divide among 2 bowls, and serve.

PER PORTION: 490 calories • 14 g protein • 13 g fat • 81 g carbohydrates

Fruited
with protein-rich Special K
Cottage Cheese

Place the cottage cheese in a bowl. Add the orange juice and beat well for a few minutes with a mixer. Add the yeast flakes and wheat germ, and stir until smooth.

Wash and peel the carrot, then grate it coarsely. Stir the grated carrot into the cottage cheese mixture. Chop the melon and stir it into the mixture. Stir in the Special K or other cereal. Spoon the mixture into bowls and serve immediately.

Serves 2:
8 oz low-fat cottage cheese
1/2 cup orange juice
1 tbs yeast flakes
1 tbs wheat germ
1 baby carrot
10 oz melon (peeled)
6-8 tbs Special K cereal, or any other low-sugar, crunchy cereal, such as corn flakes

* Power pack for the skin

Everything you eat affects your appearance. Wheat germ contains vitamins E, B_1, B_6, and folic acid, as well as magnesium, iron, and zinc. Raw grains contain a substance called *phytin*, which hinders mineral absorption; to prevent this, grains should be first soaked and boiled. Bee pollen contains concentrated nutrients, enzymes, and bioactive substances. Yogurt contains active bacteria which helps the digestive system.

PER PORTION:

270 calories

25 g protein

4 g fat

35 g carbohydrates

power

Lime-Marinated
with tomatoes, ginger, and fresh herbs
Ceviche

To make the marinade, mix together the lime juice and vinegar in a wide, shallow bowl. Wash the fish and pat dry with paper towels. Cut it into small pieces. Place the fish in the marinade, turning occasionally.

Wash and halve the tomatoes, remove the stalks and cores, and dice. Set the tomatoes aside, but transfer any seeds and juice that have escaped to the bowl with the fish. Peel the onion and slice thinly. Wash the herbs and shake dry. Remove the herb leaves from the stalks, and chop them finely. Peel and finely chop the ginger.

Spread the onion slices over a plate, followed by the diced tomato and the fish; sprinkle with the herbs. Sprinkle each layer with a little salt, pepper, marinade, and oil, and top with the chopped ginger. Serve with the bread.

Serves 2:
Juice of 1 lime
2 tbs cider vinegar
7 oz fish fillets, such as snapper or sole
2 large, ripe tomatoes
1 small sweet onion
1 bunch fresh cilantro or Italian parsley
Walnut-sized piece fresh ginger
Sea salt to taste
Black pepper to taste
1 tsp black cumin oil
Thinly sliced bread for accompaniment

Bounty from the sea

The more natural the state of the fish and vegetables you eat, the better they are for you. Don't discard the tomato seeds—they provide fiber, and cleanse your body from within. Tomatoes' best nutrients are right below the skin. Fish "cooked" in citrus juice instead of over heat retains its natural iodine and omega-3 fatty acids.

PER PORTION:

150 calories

19 g protein

5 g fat

8 g carbohydrates

Asparagus and
with spicy nori
Mushroom Salad

Serves 2:
6 tbs cider vinegar
1 tbs freshly grated
horseradish
2 tbs canola oil
2 tbs soy sauce
Black pepper to taste
6 tbs water or white wine
10 oz thick asparagus
4 oz large mushrooms
2 sheets nori
1 tbs sesame seeds
Sourdough rye bread for
accompaniment

To make the dressing, stir together the vinegar, horseradish, oil, soy sauce, pepper, and water or wine. Wash and trim the asparagus. Carefully peel the lower third of the stalks, then slice thinly. Trim the mushrooms, rinse quickly, and cut into thin slices. Cut the nori sheets into 11/2-inch pieces. Line 2 large plates with half of the nori, and drizzle with a little of the dressing. Divide the sliced asparagus, mushrooms, and the remaining nori among the plates, then drizzle with the remaining dressing. Toast the sesame seeds in a dry nonstick skillet, tossing occasionally, until you begin to smell them, and sprinkle over the salad. Let the salad stand for 30 minutes, then serve with the bread.

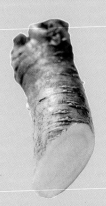

Horseradish

Horseradish contains mustard oil, which has natural antibiotic properties that support stomach acid. It also stimulates the digestive juices. Horseradish contains even more vitamin C than red bell peppers.

PER PORTION:

160 calories

5 g protein

10 g fat

8 g carbohydrates

power

Roast Beef

with arugula and pumpkin seeds

Carpaccio

To make the dressing, place the pumpkin seed and wheat germ oils, orange juice, salt, pepper, and mustard in a bowl, and whisk well. Thoroughly wash the arugula, pick over, and drain well.

Divide half of the arugula among 2 plates, and drizzle with a little of the dressing. Then, arrange the roast beef and remaining arugula leaves on top, and drizzle with the remaining dressing.

Coarsely chop the pumpkin seeds and sprinkle over the salad. Let the ingredients stand for about 30 minutes to blend the flavors. Serve with the bread.

Serves 2:

2 tbs pumpkin seed oil
1 tbs wheat germ oil
1/2 cup orange juice
Sea salt to taste
Black pepper to taste
1 tsp dry mustard
4 oz arugula
6 oz rare roast beef, very thinly sliced
2 tbs pumpkin seeds
Ciabatta or baguette for accompaniment

Dry mustard

Made of ground mustard seeds, dry mustard adds a gentle spiciness to salad dressings and marinades without adding acidity. Mustard aids digestion, is antibacterial, and promotes blood flow to the body's tissues. It is also good for indigestion. You can use prepared mustard as a substitute.

PER PORTION:

340 calories

23 g protein

23 g fat

11 g carbohydrates

Artichokes with
with basil and black cumin oil
Avocado Dip

Serves 2:
2 large artichokes
2 cups water
Pinch of sugar
Dash of cider vinegar
1 bunch fresh basil
1 ripe avocado
2 tbs fresh lemon juice
1 tsp black cumin oil
Sea salt to taste
White pepper to taste

Wash the artichokes. Break off the stalks, remove the outer leaves, and cut off any sharp tips. Bring the water to a boil with the sugar and vinegar. Cook the artichokes in the boiling water for about 30 minutes, until you can easily pull out a leaf. Remove the artichokes and reserve the cooking liquid. Wash and shake dry the basil, and remove the leaves from the stalks. Halve the avocado, and remove the pit. In a blender, puree the avocado flesh with a little of the artichoke cooking liquid and the lemon juice. Stir in the oil. Season the dip with salt and pepper, and serve as an accompaniment to the warm or cooled artichokes.

Versatile artichokes

Artichokes contain a substance called *cynarine*, which stimulates the liver and thereby cleanses the blood. It also encourages cell renewal, which makes the skin radiant. Beta-carotene and vitamin E aid this effect. You can add honey to the cooking liquid, then refrigerate it and serve as an unusual apéritif.

PER PORTION:

180 calories

5 g protein

14 g fat

11 g carbohydrates

power

Grapefruit and
with red lentils and sea vegetables
Carrot Salad

Serves 2:

2 tbs arame or dulse
1 1/2 cups water
3/4 cup red lentils
Sea salt to taste
1 tsp powdered ginger
7 oz baby carrots
7 oz spinach
1 small onion
1 pink grapefruit
3 tbs wheat germ oil
1 tsp dry mustard
Black pepper to taste
Hot cooked rice for accompaniment

In a saucepan, soak the arame or dulse in the water for 5 minutes. Add the red lentils, salt, and ginger. Cover tightly and simmer over low heat for 10 minutes; remove from the heat to prevent the sea vegetables from absorbing too much liquid. Meanwhile, wash and peel the carrots, and grate them coarsely. Wash and pick over the spinach, remove any coarse stalks, and cut the leaves into strips. Peel and finely chop the onion. Halve the grapefruit and use a spoon to scoop out segments of the flesh. Squeeze the juice from the grapefruit halves. Add the juice, grapefruit pieces, wheat germ oil, and dry mustard to the lentil and sea vegetables mixture, and carefully stir in the grated carrot and spinach strips. Season well with salt and pepper, and serve warm, accompanied by the rice.

Grapefruit

Just one grapefruit provides an adult's daily vitamin C requirement. It also stimulates the circulatory system, contributing to skin radiance.

PER PORTION:

440 calories

22 g protein

17 g fat

51 g carbohydrates

Broccoli and
with lots of vitamin E
Sauerkraut Salad

Wash the broccoli florets and drain in a strainer. Chop them a little, then puree in a blender, adding a little water to achieve a smooth texture. Drain the corn in the strainer. Coarsely chop the sauerkraut with a knife, then add it to a bowl with the corn and pureed broccoli, mixing well. Coarsely chop the sunflower kernels. Peel and finely chop the garlic.

To make the dressing, place the sunflower kernels, garlic, yogurt, oil, and vinegar in a bowl, and mix well. Season with the salt, pepper, thyme, and ginger. Pour the dressing over the vegetables and toss well. Arrange the salad on plates, and serve with bread or potatoes.

Serves 2:

5 oz broccoli florets

1-2 tbs water

1 can sweet corn kernels (7 oz)

8 oz sauerkraut (drained)

2 tbs sunflower kernels

1 clove garlic

2/3 cup plain yogurt

2 tbs nut oil

1-2 tbs cider vinegar

Sea salt to taste

Black pepper to taste

1 tsp fresh thyme leaves

1/2 tsp powdered ginger

Crusty bread or boiled small potatoes for accompaniment

Sauerkraut

Sauerkraut contains lactic acid, potassium, calcium, and iodine, as well as vitamin C. It aids digestion, and strengthens tissues. Fresh sauerkraut (non-canned) from a delicatessen is especially effective for enhancing beauty.

PER PORTION:

355 calories

11 g protein

23 g fat

31 g carbohydrates

power

Melon Puree
and fresh berries
with Fruited Risotto

Heat the oil in a pan over low heat. Add the rice and the pine nuts, and gently sauté until the rice becomes slightly translucent. Pour in half of the juice and simmer gently, stirring continuously, until the rice texture starts to become grainy. Add the remaining juice, and bring to a boil again briefly. Remove the pan from the heat, cover tightly, and let stand until cool. Refrigerate the mixture until ready to serve, up to overnight.

Cut the melon into chunks. In a blender, puree the melon flesh with the honey. Wash the berries and cut into bite-sized pieces, if necessary. Pour the melon puree into deep bowls and stir in the berries, dividing evenly. Top each serving with a scoop of the rice and serve.

Serves 2:
1 tsp wheat germ oil
1/2 cup Arborio rice
2 tbs pine nuts
1 1/2 cups apple, orange, or grape juice
12 oz cantaloupe (peeled)
1 tbs honey
1 cup fresh seasonal berries

✳ Multi-vitamin fruit juices
Some fruit juices contain added vitamins, such as A, C, and E. The primary function of these health-promoting beverages is cell protection.

PER PORTION:

425 calories

7 g protein

6 g fat

84 g carbohydrates

Fruit Salad
and toasted buckwheat
with Grapes

Serves 2: 7 oz seedless grapes • 1 apple • 1 orange • 2 tbs raisins • 1/2 cup apple, orange, or grape juice • 2 oz buckwheat groats • 2 tbs sesame seeds

Wash the fruit. Remove the grapes from the stalks. Cut the apple into eighths, remove the core, and cut each piece in half. Peel the orange, divide into segments, and cut into thirds. Place the fruit in a bowl with the raisins and juice. Toast the buckwheat and sesame seeds in a dry nonstick skillet, tossing occasionally, until you begin to smell them. Cool slightly, then sprinkle over the fruit.

PER PORTION: 295 calories • 6 g protein • 5 g fat • 60 g carbohydrates

Orange and Carrot
with high-vitamin-C rosehip extract
Cottage Cheese

Serves 2: 2 small carrots • 1 orange • 1 tbs rosehip extract • 1-2 tbs honey • 8 oz low-fat cottage cheese • 1 tsp bee pollen • 1 oz sliced almonds

Wash, peel, and finely grate the carrots. Peel the orange and cut into slices, then cut each slice into eighths. In a bowl, mix the rosehip extract with the honey, then gradually add the cottage cheese and bee pollen, mixing well. Stir in the grated carrot, orange pieces with juice, and the almonds.

PER PORTION: 200 calories • 17 g protein • 6 g fat • 20 g carbohydrates

Choco-
with dried dates
Risotto

Rinse the dates and chop into small pieces. Place the rice in a saucepan and warm gently over low heat, then pour in the milk. Add the chopped dates, cocoa powder, and honey.

Cover tightly and simmer gently over low heat for about 50 minutes, stirring occasionally, until the liquid has been absorbed. Remove the pan from the heat and let the rice cool completely.

Beat the cream until stiff peaks form. Gently mix it with the rice and serve immediately.

Serves 2:

4 oz pitted dried dates

3/4 cup Arborio rice

2 1/2 cups low-fat milk

1 tbs cocoa powder

1-2 tbs honey

1/2 cup heavy cream

Dates

These dried fruits contain good amounts of iron and potassium. Because they are naturally sweet, they are an ideal substitute for sugar. Dates are also high in fiber, which gently stimulates digestion.

PER PORTION:

560 calories

10 g protein

18 g fat

87 g carbohydrates

Green Bean and
with vitamin-packed sea vegetables
Shrimp Salad

Soak the arame or dulse in the water for 5 minutes. Meanwhile, wash and trim the beans, and remove any strings. Peel, halve, and finely chop the onion. In a skillet, heat the oil over medium heat. Add the onion and beans and sauté until the onion is translucent. Add the arame or dulse with the soaking water, and season the vegetables with salt and pepper. Add the thyme and simmer everything gently for about 15 minutes, until the beans are tender-crisp. Let the mixture cool.

Wash the tomatoes, remove the cores, and cut them into thin wedges. Cut the olives into thin slices. Drain the shrimp, if necessary, and add to the bean mixture along with the tomatoes and olives. Stir in the cider vinegar to taste.

Serves 2:
2 tbs arame or dulse
1 1/2 cups water
10 oz fresh green beans
1 small onion
1 tbs olive oil
Sea salt to taste
Black pepper to taste
1 tsp fresh thyme leaves
7 oz tomatoes
10 black olives (pitted)
7 oz small peeled cooked shrimp
2–3 tbs cider vinegar

Olives & olive oil – a healthy duo

Olives are good for the circulation, and stabilize blood pressure. They contain lactic acid, which is full of unsaturated fatty acids. Another beauty-enhancing substance in olive products is *squalene*, which keeps the skin healthy and smooth, and stimulates the immune system.

PER PORTION:

225 calories

23 g protein

9 g fat

14 g carbohydrates

Cabbage and

with fresh dill and walnuts

Apple Salad

Wash the cabbage and apples. Cut the cabbage into quarters, remove the core, and finely slice the cabbage pieces. Dry the apples and grate them coarsely without peeling them. In a bowl, mix together the sliced cabbage and grated apple. Stir the sauerkraut juice and lemon juice into the apple and cabbage mixture. Season well with salt and pepper. Let the mixture stand for about 1 hour to develop the flavors.

Meanwhile, wash the dill and shake dry. Remove the leaves from the stalks, and chop the leaves. Coarsely chop the walnuts.

To make the dressing, stir together the sour cream, chopped dill, walnuts, anise seeds, and wheat germ oil, and season with salt and pepper. Stir the dressing into the salad, seasoning again with salt and pepper to taste.

Serves 2:

7 oz white cabbage
2 sweet apples
1/2 cup sauerkraut juice
2–3 tbs fresh lemon juice
Sea salt to taste
Black pepper to taste
1/2 bunch fresh dill
2 oz walnuts
3/4 cup sour cream
1/2 tsp anise seeds

* Tough company

If the cabbage you're using seems a little too firm or tough, heat the sauerkraut and lemon juices before pouring them over the cabbage. Let the mixture stand for about 1 hour until cool; then, mix in the grated apple and remaining ingredients.

PER PORTION:

425 calories

9 g protein

32 g fat

24 g carbohydrates

Bulgur Salad
contains lots of lactic acid
with Garlic

Peel the garlic and cut into thin slices. Pour the stock into a saucepan, add the garlic, and bring to a boil. Add the bulgur wheat, season with salt and pepper, and simmer gently for about 5 minutes over low heat. Let cool.

Meanwhile, halve the bell pepper, and remove the stem, ribs, and seeds. Rinse off the pepper segments, cut them lengthwise into strips, then cut the strips into squares. Wash and shake dry the parsley, pull the leaves from the stalks, and coarsely chop the leaves. Add the bell pepper, parsley, olive oil, borage oil, and capers to the bulgur and mix well.

Finely crumble the feta cheese over the bulgur mixture. Mix and season well with salt and pepper, adding a little more stock if the salad needs moistening. Arrange on plates and serve.

Serves 2:

4 cloves garlic

1 1/4 cups vegetable stock (plus more if necessary)

4 oz bulgur wheat

Sea salt to taste

Black pepper to taste

1 red bell pepper

2 bunches fresh Italian parsley

1 tbs olive oil

1 tsp borage oil

2 tbs capers (drained)

4 oz feta cheese

Bulgur

Bulgur is crushed dried wheat, which cooks up like rice. You will find it in most health-food stores and supermarkets. It contains large amounts of protein and B-complex vitamins.

PER PORTION:

470 calories

23 g protein

19 g fat

55 g carbohydrates

Goat Cheese

with cucumber and borage oil

Sandwich

Peel and halve the cucumber, and scoop out the seeds with a spoon. Grate half of the cucumber; cut the other half into fairly thin slices. Peel and finely chop the onion. Wash and shake dry the borage or watercress, then finely chop.

In a bowl, mix the borage oil, onion, borage leaves or watercress, grated cucumber, and goat cheese until the mixture is smooth.

Spread the cheese mixture over 2 slices of the bread, dividing evenly, and top with the sliced cucumber, pressing down slightly. Season with salt and pepper, sprinkle with the sunflower kernels, and serve open-faced, or topped with 2 additional bread slices for a brown-bag lunch.

Serves 2:

1/2 cucumber
1 small onion
A few fresh borage leaves or watercress sprigs
2 tbs borage oil
4 oz soft goat cheese
2-4 slices whole wheat bread
Sea salt to taste
Black pepper to taste
1 tbs sunflower kernels

Goat cheese

Goat cheese contains less cholesterol than other types of cheese—keeping the circulatory system healthy—and is easier to digest than cow's milk cheese. It also contains lots of vitamin A, which keeps the skin smooth and the eyes shining.

PER PORTION:

305 calories

17 g protein

19 g fat

16 g carbohydrates

Salmon and Cress
fights skin irritations
Sandwich

Serves 2: 2 whole-grain rolls • 1 bunch peppercress • 1/4 cup crème fraîche • 1 tsp borage oil • Sea salt to taste • Black pepper to taste • 1 tsp fresh lemon juice • 4 slices smoked salmon

Cut the rolls in half. Rinse the cress under cold running water, and snip off the leaves, reserving some for garnish. Mix the cress with the crème fraîche, borage oil, salt, pepper, and lemon juice, and spread on the halved rolls. Top with the smoked salmon slices, dividing evenly, and garnish with the remaining cress.

PER PORTION: 330 calories • 22 g protein • 17 g fat • 22 g carbohydrates

Dry-Cured Beef
with sauerkraut and horseradish
Sandwich

Serves 2: 2 tbs grated horseradish • 1/4 cup cottage cheese • 1 tsp pumpkin seed oil • 1 tbs chopped pumpkin seeds • 2 slices seeded bread • Black pepper to taste • 2 oz sauerkraut (drained) • 6 slices dry-cured beef (such as Swiss Bundnerfleisch)

Mix the horseradish, cottage cheese, oil, and pumpkin seeds. Spread over the bread, dividing evenly, and sprinkle with pepper. Chop the sauerkraut and divide over the cottage cheese. Fold the meat slices in half and arrange on the sauerkraut.

PER PORTION: 230 calories • 18 g protein • 9 g fat • 17 g carbohydrates

Tuna and Egg
with capers and olive oil
Sandwich

Serves 2: 1 can tuna (6 oz) • 3 tbs olive oil • 1 hard-boiled egg (peeled) • 1 tbs fresh lemon juice • 2 tbs

capers • Black pepper to taste • Worcestershire sauce to taste • 2 whole-wheat rolls • 2-3 leaves radicchio

Drain the tuna. In a blender, blend the tuna, egg yolk, and lemon juice to a paste. Pour into a

bowl and stir in the capers, pepper, and Worcestershire. Halve the rolls and spread with the tuna

paste. Wash and dry the radicchio, cut into strips, and arrange on the rolls. Chop the egg white

and sprinkle over the tops.

PER PORTION: 515 calories • 27 g protein • 33 g fat • 28 g carbohydrates

Pesto-Mozzarella
with rye bread and fresh basil
Sandwich

Serves 2: 2 slices rye bread • 2 tsp prepared pesto • 1 tbs sesame seeds • 1/2 bunch fresh basil

• 6 oz fresh mozzarella cheese • 8 cherry tomatoes • Freshly ground black pepper to taste

Spread the bread with the pesto, and sprinkle with the sesame seeds. Wash and shake dry the

basil, remove the leaves from the stalks, and divide the leaves among the bread slices. Drain the

mozzarella, cut into slices, and place on top of the basil, dividing evenly. Wash and halve the

tomatoes, remove the stalks, and arrange on top of the mozzarella, dividing evenly. Sprinkle

with pepper and serve.

PER PORTION: 275 calories • 19 g protein • 16 g fat • 13 g carbohydrates

Lamb Cutlets

stimulating and full of minerals

with Vegetables

Soak the arame or dulse in 1/2 cup water for 5 minutes. Rinse and pat dry the meat. Peel and finely chop the ginger, then mix it with the dry mustard, soy sauce, lemon juice, and the 2 tablespoons water. Brush the mustard mixture over the meat. Wash and trim the remaining vegetables. Halve the leek lengthwise and slice into fine rings. Peel the carrots and cut into fine strips. Break the ends off the sugar snap peas or beans, and remove any strings.

Drain the arame or dulse well. Heat the canola oil in a nonstick skillet over medium-high heat, and brown the meat on both sides. Add the leek, carrots, peas or beans, and the arame or dulse. Season with salt and pepper, and stir-fry for about 5-7 minutes, until the meat and vegetables are cooked through. Season with soy sauce and add stir in the sesame oil. Serve with the potatoes, wild rice, or millet.

Serves 2:

2 tbs arame or dulse

1/2 cup plus 2 tablespoons water

10 oz lamb cutlets

Walnut-sized piece fresh ginger

1 tsp dry mustard

1 tbs soy sauce, plus more to taste

2 tbs fresh lemon juice

1 leek

7 oz carrots

5 oz sugar snap peas or green beans

1 tsp canola oil

Sea salt to taste

Black pepper to taste

Soy sauce to taste

1 tbs sesame oil

Cooked potatoes, wild rice, or millet, for accompaniment

PER PORTION: 330 calories • 50 g protein • 15 g fat • 43 g carbohydrates

Potato Pancake
with feta cheese and hot red chile
with Smoked Oysters

Wash the potatoes, and boil them in salted water to cover for about 10 minutes (they will be undercooked). Rinse under cold water, then peel. Cool the potatoes slightly, then grate coarsely.

Serves 2:
14 oz baking potatoes
Sea salt to taste
1 green onion
1 small red chile
1 clove garlic
3 sun-dried tomatoes
2 cans smoked oysters (3.7 oz each)
2 oz feta cheese
Black pepper to taste
Olive oil for frying

Meanwhile, wash and trim the green onion and chile. Cut the onion into thin rings, and finely chop the chile. Peel and finely chop the garlic, finely dice the tomatoes, and drain the oysters (chop them if desired). Crumble the feta cheese into a bowl, and mix with the grated potato, green onion, chile, garlic, tomatoes, and oysters. Season well with salt and pepper.

Heat 1-2 tbs olive oil in a nonstick skillet, and spread the potato-oyster mixture over the base of the skillet. Press down firmly with a spatula, cover with a lid, and fry over low heat for about 7 minutes, until golden brown. Carefully turn the pancake, and fry the other side until golden, adding more oil if necessary. Cut into wedges to serve.

Chiles
The spiciness of chile peppers stimulates digestion and circulation, and helps to prevent infection. Chile pods are incredibly hot, especially the white pith and the seeds inside. Avoid contact with the skin, particularly the nose and eyes. After handling chile peppers, wash your hands thoroughly to prevent burning, or wear plastic gloves.

PER PORTION:
560 calories
28 g protein
14 g fat
82 g carbohydrates

Mashed
with spiced herring, radishes, and fresh chives
Potatoes

Soak the Matjes in water for at least 1–2 hours. Wash the potatoes, and boil them in

salted water to cover for about 20-30 minutes, until tender.

Drain the potatoes, peel, and set aside.

Meanwhile, wash and shake dry the chives, then chop finely.

Wash the radishes, setting aside 4, plus a few of the tender

leaves, for garnish. Trim and dice the remaining radishes.

In a saucepan, heat the potatoes with the milk and canola oil

over medium heat, until just simmering. With a potato masher,

mash the potatoes coarsely. Stir in the chives and diced

radishes, season with salt and pepper, and heat through.

Remove the fish from the soaking water, pat dry, and arrange

on plates with the mashed potatoes and reserved radishes. Sprinkle the chopped

radish leaves on top, and serve.

Serves 2:
4 Matjes herring fillets
14 oz baking potatoes
Sea salt to taste
1 bunch fresh chives
1 bunch radishes
1/2 cup acidopholous milk (or more if needed)
1 tbs canola oil
White pepper to taste

Matjes

Matjes are small red herring fillets, which
have been spiced and brined. They are
particularly delicate, and contain plenty of
omega-3 fatty acids. Eating Matjes is
especially good for skin radiance.

PER PORTION:

625 calories

31 g protein

44 g fat

27 g carbohydrates

Millet Spaghetti
with saffron and sesame
with Carrots

Serves 2:

9 oz fresh, green-topped carrots
1 onion
1 clove garlic
1 tbs sesame oil
2 tbs sesame seeds
Sea salt to taste
Black pepper to taste
Small pinch of ground star anise
Pinch of powdered saffron
1/2 cup orange juice
8 oz millet spaghetti

Wash the carrots and a handful of the green tops. Trim and peel the carrots, and slice them into long strips with a vegetable peeler. Peel and finely chop the onion and garlic. In a skillet, heat the sesame oil over medium-low heat. Add the sesame seeds and stir until light golden brown. Add the onion and garlic, and sauté over medium heat until the onion is translucent.

Add the carrot strips and season with salt, pepper, and star anise. Cover tightly and simmer gently over low heat for 1-2 minutes. In a small bowl, mix the saffron with the orange juice. Add the juice and green carrot tops to the pan, and stir. Simmer gently for another 2-3 minutes over low heat.

Meanwhile, cook the pasta in plenty of boiling salted water until slightly firm to the bite (*al dente*). Drain, and mix with the cooked carrot mixture. Arrange on plates and serve immediately.

PER PORTION: 560 calories • 22 g protein • 11 g fat • 93 g carbohydrates

Pasta and
with blue cheese-tomato sauce
Sea Vegetables

Soak the arame or dulse in the water for 5 minutes. Meanwhile, cut an X into the round ends of the tomatoes and plunge them into boiling water for a few moments. Remove the skins and

Serves 2:

2 tbs arame or dulse

1 cup water

1 lb ripe tomatoes

1 onion

2 tbs wheat germ oil

2 tbs tomato paste

Sea salt to taste

8 oz millet spaghetti

1-2 tbs lemon juice

5 oz blue cheese
(rind removed)

Soy sauce, black pepper, and
sweet paprika to taste

stalks, and puree in a blender. Peel and finely chop the onion. In a large rimmed skillet, heat 1 tbs of the oil over medium heat. Add the onion and sauté until translucent. Stir in the pureed tomato and tomato paste, and simmer briefly over low heat.

In a large saucepan, bring plenty of salted water to a boil. Drain the arame or dulse, and add it to the water with the spaghetti, cooking until the spaghetti is slightly firm to the bite, *al dente*. Drain, rinse under cold water, then drain again. Toss the spaghetti mixture with the lemon juice and the remaining 1 tbs oil. Crumble the cheese and melt it in the tomato sauce. Season the sauce well with soy sauce, pepper, and paprika. Add a little water to the sauce if it is too thick. Arrange the spaghetti mixture on plates, top with the sauce, and serve.

Blue cheese

Blue cheese is injected with cultures and then left to mature, until it has developed its characteristic blue-green veins. It is full of protein, easy to digest, and its enzymes have a beneficial effect on intestinal flora, and on digestion in general.

PER PORTION:

810 calories

33 g protein

43 g fat

73 g carbohydrates

Green Veggie
with appearance-enhancing asparagus
Ragout

Wash the cucumber, and cut in half lengthwise. Scoop out the seeds with a spoon, and cut into 1/2-inch slices. Wash and trim the asparagus, carefully peel the lower third of the stalks, and cut into 3/4-1-inch pieces. Trim and pick over the arugula, then wash, shake dry, and finely chop. Wash, shake dry, and pick over the spinach, break off any coarse stalks, and roughly chop. Peel and finely chop the onion and garlic. In a skillet, heat the oil over medium heat. Add the onion and garlic and sauté until translucent. Add the asparagus and the cucumber. Season with salt, pepper, and nutmeg, and cover tightly. Simmer gently for about 10 minutes over low heat. Add the spinach and the arugula, season with salt and pepper, and simmer for another 3 minutes. Divide the vegetables among serving plates, drizzle with the borage oil, and grate the cheese over the top.

Serves 2:

1 cucumber
9 oz asparagus
1 bunch fresh arugula
9 oz fresh spinach
1 onion
1 clove garlic
1 tbs olive oil
Sea salt to taste
Black pepper to taste
Ground nutmeg to taste
2 tsp borage oil
2 oz Parmesan cheese

Asparagus

Asparagus contains aspartic acid and potassium, which stimulate the kidneys and help the body to expel excess liquid (diuretic). It is also extremely low in calories, and is excellent for a weight-reducing diet, provided it is prepared with low-fat and -calorie ingredients. Although its benefits are not dependent on the variety, green asparagus contains more vitamins than the harder-to-find white.

power

PER PORTION:

215 calories

17 g protein

10 g fat

13 g carbohydrates

Boiled Potatoes with
ideal for nerves and stomach
Creamy Power Spread

Wash the potatoes and place them in a saucepan with salted water to cover. Cover the pan with a lid, bring the water to a boil, and boil for about 20 minutes, until tender. Meanwhile, halve the pepper, and remove the stem, ribs, and seeds. Rinse the pepper, then cut into small squares. Peel and finely chop the shallot and garlic. Wash and shake dry the parsley, remove the leaves from the stalks, and finely chop. Place the cream cheese in a bowl and mix with the parsley, wheat germ, yeast flakes, flaxseed oil, Tabasco, and enough water to make a smooth mixture. Mix in the chopped bell pepper, the diced shallot, and the garlic. Season well, and serve with the warm drained potatoes.

Serves 2:

1 lb small red-skinned potatoes
Sea salt to taste
1 small red bell pepper
1 shallot
1 clove garlic
1 bunch fresh Italian parsley
8 oz low-fat cream cheese
1 tbs wheat germ
1 tbs yeast flakes
1 tbs flaxseed oil
Tabasco sauce to taste
About 1/2 cup spring water

Potatoes–getting down to the roots

Potatoes contain plenty of valuable plant protein and vitamin C, and are thus an important ingredient in a powerfood plan. Raw potato juice, which is available from health-food stores, is excellent for the stomach, and is an ideal remedy for over-acidity in the system. Served with cream cheese, potatoes are similar in nutrients to a small steak, and the fiber they contain stimulates the digestion. Do not eat uncooked potatoes, as they contain indigestible starches.

PER PORTION:

335 calories
25 g protein
9 g fat
41 g carbohydrates

Turkey Breast
tender and mildly spicy
with Endive

Cut the turkey breast against the grain into 1/2-inch slices. Season with salt, pepper, and paprika. Wash and trim the endive, and cut in half lengthwise. In a saucepan, melt the butter over medium-high heat and sauté the endive until just brown at the edges. Add the turkey and brown on all sides. Add the tomatoes and season with salt and pepper. Cover tightly and simmer gently for 5 minutes over low heat. Meanwhile, peel the ginger and garlic, and slice them thinly. Add them to the skillet along with the bean sprouts and sesame oil. Drain the mozzarella, cut into slices, and place on the endive. Simmer gently over low heat until the cheese melts. Arrange on plates and serve accompanied by the baguette.

Serves 2:

7 oz boneless turkey breast
Sea salt to taste
Black pepper to taste
Sweet paprika to taste
2 heads Belgian endive
1 tsp butter
1/2 can (14.5 oz can) diced tomatoes
Walnut-sized piece fresh ginger
1 clove garlic
4 oz bean sprouts
1 tbs sesame oil
4 oz fresh mozzarella cheese
Baguette for accompaniment

Belgian endive

Endive's bitter constituents stimulate the stomach, spleen, liver, and gall bladder, making it a veritable spa food. Its components—including special carbohydrates known as "fos" (*fructooligosaccharides*)—influence intestinal health and help regenerate the membranes and flora of the intestine.

PER PORTION:

350 calories

40 g protein

17 g fat

10 g carbohydrates

Spicy Beef Stir-Fry
spicy and wonderfully stimulating
with Avocado

Combine the lemon juice, salt, pepper, a pinch of paprika, and the star anise in a shallow bowl. Cut the meat into thin strips against the grain, and place in the bowl, turning to coat the meat. Slit open the chile, remove the stem and seeds, rinse, and finely chop. Halve the bell pepper, remove the stem, ribs, and seeds, rinse, and coarsely chop. Peel and finely chop the garlic and onion.

Drain the meat. In a wok or large skillet, heat the oil over medium-high heat, add the meat, and brown on all sides. Add the chile, a pinch of paprika, the garlic and onion, and stir-fry for 5 minutes. Wash and shake dry the parsley, remove the leaves from the stalks, and chop. Halve the avocado, remove the pit, and chop. Mix the avocado, olives, and parsley, and season to taste with lemon juice, salt, and pepper. Divide the beef mixture among serving dishes, top with the avocado mixture, and serve with the desired accompaniment.

Serves 2:

3 tbs fresh lemon juice, plus more to taste

Sea salt to taste

Black pepper to taste

Hot paprika

1/2 tsp ground star anise

7 oz lean beef

1 small red or green chile

1 green bell pepper

2 cloves garlic

1 onion

1-2 tbs olive oil

1 bunch fresh Italian parsley

1 avocado

10 black olives (pitted)

Boiled millet, brown rice, or crusty bread for accompaniment

PER PORTION:

390 calories

26 g protein

26 g fat

17 g carbohydrates

Avocado

Avocado is a tonic for the stomach, nerves, skin, and hair—provided it is ripe, and as soft as butter. Avocado contains valuable plant oils, and lots of B-complex vitamins. Mashed with a few drops of lemon juice, salt, and pepper, it makes an ideal spread, dip, or sauce.

Salmon
with feta and fresh dill
on Fennel

Serves 2:
2 small salmon fillets
(about 7 oz each)
2 tbs cider vinegar
Sea salt to taste
Black pepper to taste
1 small bulb fennel
14 oz baking potatoes
1/2 bunch fresh dill
1 tbs wheat germ oil
1/2 cup plus 2 tbs water
1 tbs fennel seeds
4 oz feta cheese

Wash and pat dry the salmon fillets. Sprinkle them with the vinegar, then season with salt and pepper. Wash and trim the fennel, and cut into thin slices. Reserve a little of the green fennel tops. Wash and peel the potatoes, and cut into 1/2-inch cubes. Wash and shake dry the dill, remove the leaves from the stalks, and combine with the reserved fennel tops. In a saucepan, heat the oil over medium heat. Add the fennel and sauté for 2-3 minutes. Add the potatoes, and season with salt and pepper. Add the water and fennel seeds, and simmer for 5 minutes. Sprinkle the dill and fennel leaf mixture over the fish, and place the fish in the pan on top of the potato mixture. Crumble the feta over the top, cover tightly, and simmer everything gently for another 15 minutes, until the potatoes and fish are cooked through. Check periodically to see that there is still liquid in the pan.

Cider vinegar–modern medicine

There's a good reason why cider vinegar is currently so popular: it fights putrefactive bacteria in the intestine, kills germs, aids detoxification, and improves digestion. It is also slightly milder than wine vinegar, so it is excellent in the kitchen.

PER PORTION:
525 calories
55g protein
20 g fat
28 g carbohydrates

Sweet and Sour
with coconut and pineapple
Shrimp Fried Rice

In a saucepan, stir the rice over medium-high heat until slightly toasted. Add the water and salt, and bring to a boil. Cover tightly and simmer over low heat for 20 minutes, until the liquid is absorbed. Meanwhile, wash, trim, and peel the carrots, then cut into slices. Halve the bell pepper, remove the stem, ribs, and seeds, rinse, and cut into squares. Trim the green onion and cut into thin rings.

Peel the ginger and cut into very thin strips. Peel and halve the pineapple, remove the brown "eyes" and core, and chop the flesh.

In a wok or large skillet, heat the oil over medium-high heat. Add the carrots, pepper, and green onion, and stir-fry briefly, then gradually add the coconut, ginger, and bean sprouts, stirring continuously. Add the cooked rice, pineapple, and the shrimp, and stir-fry until the shrimp just turns opaque. Season with soy sauce and serve immediately.

Serves 2:
1/2 cup brown basmati rice
1 cup water
1 tsp sea salt
2 small carrots
1/2 red bell pepper
1 green onion
Walnut-sized piece fresh ginger
1 small, or 1/4 large fresh pineapple
1-2 tbs canola oil
3 tbs grated unsweetened coconut
4 oz bean sprouts
6 oz shrimp, peeled and deveined
Soy sauce to taste

Sprouted soybeans

Sprouting improves the constituents of the soybean: it increases the vitamin content, breaks down protein, makes the fat more digestible, and encourages the growth of enzymes. After sprouting, the calorie content also drops.

PER PORTION:

600 calories

26 g protein

24 g fat

70 g carbohydrates

Radicchio and

with lentils and prunes

Fish Stew

Wash and pat dry the fish fillets, drizzle with cider vinegar, and season with salt. Trim the leek and slit it open lengthwise. Wash it well and cut into thin slices. Cut the prunes lengthwise into quarters. In a skillet, heat the oil over medium heat. Add the leek and sauté until glazed. Add the stock, salt, bay leaf, peppercorns, cloves, prunes, and lentils. Cover tightly and simmer over low heat for about 8 minutes; the lentils will still be slightly firm. Meanwhile, trim and wash the radicchio, and cut the leaves into strips. Add the radicchio and the fish, with the marinade, to the lentils, and simmer gently for another 3-4 minutes over low heat.

Stir in the honey and season with salt. Arrange on plates and serve with the baguette.

Serves 2:

10 oz mild white fish fillets

3 tbs cider vinegar

Sea salt to taste

1 leek

10 prunes (pitted)

1 tbs canola oil

2 1/2 cups fish or vegetable stock

1 bay leaf

3 peppercorns

2 whole cloves

2/3 cup French green lentils

1 head radicchio (about 5 oz)

1 tsp honey

Baguette for accompaniment

Radicchio

Radicchio tastes—and works—like the bitters you might find in a bar. Raddichio's constituents stimulate the digestion, and at the same time are soothing and cleanse the blood. Radicchio is related to, and is just as calming, as endive (see page 50). It's only drawback it that it loses much of its lovely red color when cooked.

PER PORTION:

525 calories

43 g protein

9 g fat

65 g carbohydrates

Chinese
Fondue

with fresh fish and vegetables

Wash and pat dry the fish, and cut it crosswise into 1¼-inch strips. Then, cut each strip into 1½-inch pieces. Peel and finely chop the ginger. Trim, wash, and thinly slice the green onion. Squeeze the juice from the lime and reserve 1 teaspoon of the juice. Mix the remaining juice with the ginger and sliced green onion. Drizzle the ginger mixture over the fish, season with salt and pepper, and refrigerate until ready to eat. Wash and trim the sugar snap peas, and slice them on the diagonal. Wipe clean the mushrooms. Wash and halve the bell pepper, then remove the stem, ribs, and seeds. Slice the pepper on the diagonal. Put the sugar snap peas, mushrooms, and bell pepper in the refrigerator until ready to eat.

At serving time, heat the stock with the remaining 1 teaspoon lime juice and the lemon grass, until simmering. Light the heat source for the fondue pot. Pour the stock into the fondue pot, and place over the heat source. Put the fish and the vegetables in bowls around the fondue pot. Using fondue forks or small skimmers, cook the fish and vegetables in the stock and eat immediately. Accompany with rice, soy sauce, and sauces of your choice.

Serves 2:

14 oz Norwegian salmon-trout (arctic char) fillets
Walnut-sized piece fresh ginger
1 green onion
1 lime
Sea salt to taste
Black pepper to taste
7 oz sugar snap peas
7 oz small white or shiitake mushrooms
1 red bell pepper
1 1/2 quarts chicken stock
2-3 stalks lemon grass
Hot cooked rice, soy sauce, and dipping sauces of your choice as accompaniments

PER PORTION: 315 calories • 65 g protein • 10 g fat • 52 g carbohydrates

Eggplant and
with spicy tomato sauce
Shrimp Roll-Ups

Wash the eggplant, remove the stalk, and cut in on the diagonal into thin slices. Sprinkle the slices with salt, pile the slices into two equal stacks, and weight them down with a cutting board. Rinse and drain the shrimp. Cut open the chile lengthwise, remove the seeds, then rinse and chop finely. Trim and finely chop the shallot. Peel and finely chop the garlic. Combine half each of the chile, shallot, and garlic with the lemon juice and 1 tbs of the oil, and drizzle over the shrimp. Cut an X into the round ends of the tomatoes and plunge them into boiling water for a few moments. Remove the skins, cut the tomatoes in half, remove the seeds, and chop coarsely. Mix the tomatoes with the remaining chile mixture, the honey, and black cumin oil, and season with salt and pepper.

Squeeze the liquid from the eggplant, wipe dry each slice with paper towels, and brush with pesto. Place the eggplant and the shrimp on a hot griddle or flat skillet, and brown on both sides; the shrimp is done when it just turns opaque. Roll the shrimp in the eggplant slices and serve with the tomato mixture and bread.

Serves 2:
1 small eggplant (about 7 oz)
Sea salt to taste
8 jumbo shrimp, peeled and deveined
1 red chile
1 shallot
1 clove garlic
Juice of 1/2 lemon
2 tbs olive oil
7 oz tomatoes
1 tsp honey
1 tsp black cumin oil
1 tsp prepared pesto
Crusty bread as accompaniment

Good options
You could also cook this dish on a grill, or under the broiler. Marinated salmon-trout (page 57) or beef (page 51) are excellent alternatives to the shrimp.

PER PORTION:

180 calories

10 g protein

12 g fat

8 g carbohydrates

Steamed Fresh
in a creamy broth
Mussels

Wash the mussels, scrubbing them thoroughly, and carefully remove any attached hairy filaments (beards). Discard any shells that are open.

Peel the onion and slice into rings. Trim and wash the celery, and cut into slices.

In a large skillet, heat the oil over medium heat. Add the onion, and sauté until translucent. Add the celery, and sauté briefly. Peel and crush the garlic, and add it to the skillet. Add the mussels and vegetable stock, and bring to a boil. Cover tightly and cook for about 8 minutes. Remove the mussels when all the shells have opened, and keep warm.

Serves 2:

2 lb mussels

1 onion

1-2 stalks celery

1 tbs canola oil

1 clove garlic

2 cups vegetable stock

1/3 cup sour cream

Sea salt to taste

Black pepper to taste

1/2 bunch fresh Italian parsley

Crusty bread for accompaniment

Pass the mussel cooking liquid through a fine strainer into a clean saucepan, and cook over high heat until reduced to about a third of the original volume. Stir in the sour cream and just heat through. Season with salt and pepper.

Wash and shake dry the parsley, remove the leaves from the stalks, and chop the leaves. Sprinkle the parsley over the sauce. Return the mussels to the broth, and accompany with the bread for dipping.

power

PER PORTION: 225 calories • 15 g protein • 15 g fat • 8 g carbohydrates

Index

Abbreviations

tsp = teaspoon
tbs = tablespoon

Published originally under the title
BEAUTY FOOD: Natürliche Schönheit für
Haut und Haar

©1999 Gräfe und Unzer Verlag GmbH,
Munich
English translation copyright for the US
edition: © 2000 Silverback Books, Inc.

Editors: Ina Schröter, Jennifer Newens, CCP
Readers: Dipl. oec. troph. Maryna Zimdars,
Vené Franco
Layout and design: Heinz Kraxenberger
Production: Helmut Giersberg,
Shanti Nelson
Photos: FoodPhotography Eising, Munich
Typeset: Easy Pic Library, Munich
Reproduction: Repro Schmidt, Dornbirn
Printing: Appl, Wemding
Binding: Sellier, Freising

ISBN: 1-930603-20-7

Caution
The techniques and recipes in this book are
to be used at the reader's sole discretion
and risk. Always consult a doctor before
beginning a new eating plan.

Dagmar von Cramm
Studied ecotrophology, and after graduation
began to practice nutritional theory in
cooking. The mother of three sons, she has
been a freelance food journalist since 1984.
She has been a member of the Presiding
Committee of the German Society for
Nutrition since 1996.

Susie M. and **Pete Eising** have studios in
Munich and Kennebunkport, Maine/USA.
They studied at the Munich Academy of
Photography, where they established their
own studio for food photography in 1991.

For this book:
Photographic layout:
Martina Görlach
Food styling:
Monika Schuster

SILVERBACK
BOOKS, INC.